HABITATS OF THE WORLD

POLAR REGIONS

ALISON BALLANCE

DOMINIE PRESS
Pearson Learning Group

The South Pole — Antarctica

The South Pole is at the bottom of the world. It is in a place called Antarctica. Antarctica is the coldest place on earth.

The North Pole — the Arctic

The North Pole is at the top of the world in a place called the Arctic. Almost all of Antarctica is covered in ice and snow all year. The Arctic is mostly free of ice and snow in the summer.

About the Poles

During the summer, the sun shines all day and all night. Near the end of summer, the sun is low in the sky, even in the middle of the day. During the winter, there is no sun at all. It is dark for six months.

It is very windy at the **poles**.
The wind makes the cold air even
colder.

The poles are also very dry.
There is no water for animals or
people to drink.

Arctic Foxes

Animals have to be tough to **survive** near the poles. Arctic foxes have very thick fur to keep them warm. In the winter, their fur turns white like snow. They even have fur on the bottom of their feet.

Penguins

A penguin is a type of bird, but it cannot fly. Five kinds of penguins live in Antarctica. Emperor penguins are the biggest penguins. Penguins spend lots of time at sea catching fish to eat. They come ashore to lay their eggs and raise their babies, which are called **chicks**.

Seals

Seals are covered in fat, which is called **blubber**. The blubber keeps them warm. Seals swim underneath the ice. They can hold their breath for an hour.

Polar Bears

Polar bears live only in the Arctic. During the winter, they dig holes underneath the snow. These holes are called **dens**. Polar bears sleep in their dens during the whole winter. They wake up in spring, when it is warmer.

Krill

Krill are small animals that look like shrimp. They are the most **common** animals in the seas around Antarctica. Krill are very important because most Antarctic animals eat them.

Polar Plants

There are very few plants in Antarctica. They need to be tough. **Lichen** do not need soil to grow. Arctic plants have small leaves that protect them from freezing and help them to **conserve** water.

Polar Science

Nobody lives in Antarctica during the winter months. But scientists come here to visit and study lots of different things. They have to wear special, thick clothing to keep warm. They know that this is the very coldest habitat in the entire world.

GLOSSARY

blubber: A thick layer of fat that keeps an animal warm

chicks: Baby birds, such as baby penguins

common: Found in many places; numerous

conserve: To keep or save for future use

den: An animal's nest; often underground or in a cave

krill: Small animals that look like shrimp

lichen: A type of Arctic plant

poles: The northernmost and southernmost points on earth

survive: To stay alive

INDEX